MOONTOUCHED

The Poetry of K. R. Lehman

MANIC RAVEN PRESS

ISBN: 978-1-9999629-0-6

MANIC RAVEN PRESS

To all who have believed in me.
You will know who you are.

I wander the Earth with unsure feet,
In a haze of residual dreams.
From a time I can barely remember,
From the other side of the seam.
Memories vague and troubling,
I carry around like an ache;
Walking among the waking world,
As one who has yet to wake.

~New Moon~

There is
Music this night.
Do you hear it too?
The sound of a distant piano?
A mournful and haunting tune?

Listen!
On the wind!
Is that a violin?
It seems to be weeping,
So plaintive and woeful it sounds!
I could weep for hearing it,
Indeed I'm weeping now.

~Waxing Crescent~

In the fire
I lost my shape;
My life in the hands of a smith
Who, separating the poor from the pith,
Would determine the new shape I would take.

In the fire I lost who I was,
To what I would soon become.
In strange and calloused hands, undone,
And remade from the steel I possessed all along.

~First Quarter~

I just wanted to say that if...
If you need someone
To protect your light,
To carry it
And guard it...
To hold it close
And wear it well...
Wield it well...
I'm here.
I can do it.
I will do it.

~Waxing Gibbous~

What they don't know,
Is what I carry inside me.
A fragment...
That needed somewhere to go,
So I offered to take it.
What they don't know,
Is that I was starborn,
But moontouched.

~Full Moon~

I saw in the night sky a warning,
That the Earth will not be here come morning,
For our star has been slowly transforming,
And has burned its hydrogen out.

We will be slain by the giant
That we trusted; our end will be violent,
And for all that we know of science–
This we can do nothing about.

In my mind's eye I saw this occur;
Eight minutes 'til they know
On the other side of the world;
Eight minutes yet,
So quickly spread the word,
The hydrogen has finally burned out.

~Waning Gibbous~

A stranger on the doorstep
Knocked and wearily waited.
When the door swung slowly open,
He cleared his throat and straightened.
"I am in need of a shelter," he said.
"To get me out of the rain."
His voice was halting and weak,
His hair was a wet grizzled mane.
The woman in the door seemed unsure,
She peered at him very closely.
"Sir, do I know you?" she asked him then.
Something about him seemed ghostly.
He shook his head, water running down his face,
And dripping in streams from his beard.
"I'm afraid you don't," he answered her.
"I'm not from around here."
She thought for a moment, then sighed.
"I don't mean to be rude,
But I don't know you and I have a family.
I don't think letting you in would be shrewd."
The stranger nodded, "I understand."
He turned and left uncomplaining.
The woman stood and watched him go,
Only then realizing it wasn't raining.

~Last Quarter~

I am ever sobered
By the change of seasons,
For it reminds me of
My own mortality
And inevitable change.
A seriousness grows
Upon me while
The trees are robbed
Of their robes
By the thieving
Wind.

~Waning Crescent~

Mother,
This place is dark.
I don't know
Where I am.

~New Moon~

I am not so naive
In my praying
To believe that
Anyone is listening.
I am not so arrogant
As to think
That anyone cares
About me at all.

~Waxing Crescent~

The silence here is deep,
Curious, and imposing.
It stirs my mind from sleep,
Though I feel it gently closing
Around me as I keep
My fear from shame disclosing.

The darkness here is absolute,
Aphotic, yet revealing.
An awareness of something terribly acute
Rises within me; a feeling,
An understanding that my life is moot,
That my existence has no meaning.

~First Quarter~

East Wind, fill my sails
'Til they strain against the mast,
For after countless years at sea,
I have found it at last.

Blow, East Wind, blow.
Push me ever onward.
For a place of peace awaits me,
A quiet and placid harbor.

Rush me to the west, East Wind.
Get me there by gloaming.
To the haven in which I will anchor my soul,
And cease my endless roaming.

~Waxing Gibbous~

On this divinely ethereal night
My Mother-Queen, sweet satellite!
Has filled the lake with liquid light,
And I tremble barefoot on the shore.
Lapping at my toes, teasing and cool,
The water shines like a silver jewel;
Timidly I step into this magical pool,
And join the lost things at its floor!

~Full Moon~

In the quiet I search
For meaning,
In the weary sigh of the
Evening,
When the toils of the day
Are done,
And I am left again to
Dreaming.
What has this day
Accomplished?
Has it achieved
Its promise?
No, but like the days
Preceding it,
It's left me with
No solace.

~Waning Gibbous~

The air was somehow heavier
As we bore her away
To bury her
On that night of reckoning.

I felt in my bones a warning
That the morrow would
Find us mourning;
Would find us our courage questioning.

Her skin glowed pale and white,
To give us away as
We stole through the night;
To make it known the cause of her death.

The two frightened and stumbling figures
Carrying her body
With blood-slick fingers;
The two now swimming way out of their depth.

Truly a crime of passion,
We looked at her grave,
Our faces ashen,
For we had both loved her indeed.

And it should have been
Us instead of her;
Two bodies buried
Beneath the dirt,

Should've been,
Had we not been blinded
By greed.

~Last Quarter~

There is truth to the fabric of space-time,
For I have witnessed the seams;
Have fallen through gaps in the weave;
Things are much like Einstein believed.
But what he hesitated to say, perhaps,
Is that it's multi-layered and thick,
And it can be torn and ripped;
Wrinkled and stretched and stitched.

~Waning Crescent~

Days of youth,
You are gone from me now.
But I remember you fondly
And always I shall.
Now I grow old,
But unlike days bygone,
I am not afraid.
Antiquity becomes me.
It sits well with my mind.
It reflects my soul,
And my cosmic age.

~New Moon~

I chose a life of seclusion,
A hermit deep in the woods;
I hid myself in the woods,
To rid my mind of delusion,
And my ever-darkening moods.

I sought a secret knowledge,
And fanned an invisible flame;
Fed and nurtured this flame,
'Til there amongst the foliage,
I found what I'd hoped to claim.

And when this was done I returned,
To the world outside of the timber;
The world I had left for the timber,
And found that for all I had learned,
It was still the world I remembered.

~Waxing Crescent~

The air is filled
With the scent of roses,
The day sleeps
And reposes,
And love is not so much
A "How are you?"
As a "Where are you?
I need you."

~First Quarter~

Lying in my bed at night,
Lines stretch before my eyes.
Parallel planes, and symmetries;
Sacred patterns, and geometries.
I swear I have found God in these.

~Waxing Gibbous~

You are...beautiful,
More beautiful than I deserve,
Prized beyond anything
I've ever earned.
How came you to me?
To me, above all?
What divinity in heaven
Could have let you so fall?

~Full Moon~

It is night
And Luna is on
Her throne,
But I am pining
For another.
Does she know?
Does she know that
I am longing for
The warmth of
The sun on my face?
She cannot condone
Me for it.
For she, even
Now, is basking
In his glow.

~Waning Gibbous~

The first resounding note,
The stricken chord,
Arouses my senses and
Brings me back to life.
This music seems to have
Been born from my heart,
And is saying all the
Things I cannot seem
To say.

~Last Quarter~

Oh stormy life,
Oh troubled man,
Tell me which do you prefer?
The distant thunderstorm,
Or the one outside your window?
Take shelter beneath my roof.
Hide within my walls.
I will be home shortly.
Sit quietly beside the fire,
And in its glow
Ponder your life.

Fear not the thunder,
Nor heed the wind
That violently shakes the window panes.
Instead peruse my books.
Leaf through their pages.
Wander in unknown realms.

Oh stormy life,
Oh troubled man,
Tell me why are you afraid?
Do not you know that storms always pass
And thunder always silences?
Take shelter beneath my roof.
Hide away inside my walls
And I will be home shortly.

Light a cigarette from the box
That sits upon the table,
Let the world become hazy and gray.
Heed not the rain,
Nor fear the lightening
That sizzles and cracks like a whip.
Instead take down a glass,
And fill it with wine.
Sit quietly and ponder your life.
And the storm without will cease,
And I will come home,
To find the storm still raging within.

~Waning Crescent~

There is a loneliness deep within my soul,
An emptiness that cannot be made full.
I sorrow as one who has lost
That which made them whole.
I wander as one who has not
A home in all the world.

~New Moon~

And what will become of people like us?
The people who battle the constant ache,
The unrest?

Where will we find ourselves in the end?
Or will we find ourselves at all?

~Waxing Crescent~

I will love you from over here,
For it seems I must;
From over here,
Where only you can see me standing,
And when others swear they see a
Shadow move,
Only you will know it's me.

~First Quarter~

My soul is brooding
And darkly I sit
In mid-afternoon
Among the woodland phlox.

It seems unholy
To be so ill-at-ease
In such a bower,
But even here
I find no solace.

For the outside world
Has wearied me,
Beyond what our sweet Mother
Can heal.

My soul is heavy
And darkly I sit
Among the woodland phlox
In the nectar spring.

~Waxing Gibbous~

By lantern-light
I descended,
Down into the
Dark crypt,
Coming to where
The steps ended.
On the lantern
I tightened my grip,
For I saw what I
Had not intended,
Saw something
I could not predict;
Saw myself laid
Out unattended
And an elegy
Carved in mirror-script.

~Full Moon~

How is it
That others
See a light
In me
When all I feel
Is darkness?

~Waning Gibbous~

I long for you as the thirsty man
Longs for water.
The worker, for rest.
The traveler, home.

~Last Quarter~

I know nothing sweet without
A little bitterness;
Nothing happy without a tinge
Of sadness.
This melancholy is a part of me.
It accompanies everything I do.
It is my familiar and most
Faithful companion.
And I would be lost
Without it.

~Waning Crescent~

It is twilight in my soul,
The hour when things are most unclear;
When shadows like wraiths and specters appear;
When trembling is not from the cold,
But from fear;
That darkest hour of the soul.

~New Moon~

All I ever wanted was for you to see me.
Here, in the corner where I sat in silence,
Too afraid to stand up and
Throw off my shadowy mantle;
Too afraid to let the light
Fall fully across my face.
You were ever the life of the party,
Commanding attention in the center
Of the room.

Why couldn't you see me?
The intensity of my gaze
Should have been enough.
Or were you afraid of the pull
That you felt from the
Dark of the corner?

~Waxing Crescent~

I told you about my vision,
Then we sat in silence,
Each of us in our own thoughts,
For I was unable to elaborate;
Unwilling to elaborate.

~First Quarter~

I tried to walk a mile,
A mile in your shoes,
But I stumbled
And I fell
And I lay
Broken and
Bruised.

I tried to build a castle,
A castle lofty and strong,
But it crumbled
And it fell
And I lay
Buried long.

I tried to touch the sun,
The sun bright and round.
I was humbled
When I fell
And I lay
Dead on the
Ground.

~Waxing Gibbous~

It was in the month of October,
That I found at last what I'd sought.
The key to the tomb in the graveyard,
In the midst of my family's plot.
It was beneath the Hunter's Moon,
That I stole quietly to the gate;
Swinging it open and slipping through,
Closer now to the secret that waits.
It was before the tomb's ancient door
That I paused and fought with fear,
At last mastering that wise old foe,
Wondering why he chose to interfere.
It was after boldly inserting the key
Into the rusted and weather-worn lock,
And using both hands to get it to turn,
That I heard from the other side a soft knock.
It was while my heart had stopped beating
And it seemed I had ceased to breathe,
That the door of the tomb was swung open
And a figure stepped out, baring gruesome teeth.
It was in the month of October,
Beneath the Hunter's Moon,
That I released the monster
That had been locked away in the tomb.

~Full Moon~

I am moved.
Something stirs inside.
Something is happening that is bigger than me.
A fate decided.
A wheel spun.
I hear its spinning
And I am moved.

~Waning Gibbous~

Who can explain the human heart?
How it stops and how it starts!
Who can say what makes it cold and grim,
And what can make it live again?

~Last Quarter~

Time is as a river,
Ever flowing,
Ever moving,
Rushing to a specific point–
The point in which we are lost.

~Waning Crescent~

In the dark of my room,
After the door has been closed
And "good nights" exchanged customarily,
I am left with my thoughts,
With the things that I know,
And tears fall involuntarily.

There is something in my heart
That gets harbored away,
Suppressed and pushed to the side;
'Til the dark of my room
At the end of the day
Draws it like a well from my eyes.

~New Moon~

Just once,
Will you come?
When the day is done,
And I've laid my head
Upon my pillow?

Just one time,
Could you be here,
And let me lay my head
In your lap
And breathe you in?

~Waxing Crescent~

Dawn breaks
In a sky as an inverted sea,
In waves and crests of color.
The earth is bathed in light;
The earth is flooded
With light.

~First Quarter~

I always feel stronger in the morning,
Before the realization of the day has set in.
Drinking my coffee alone and in silence,
Pondering the sun's entrance on this,
My side of the world.

The birds are always happy in the morning,
Except for the mourning dove,
But that is because he is first to realize the day.

I wonder if he ever forgets it?
These are my thoughts in the morning,
As I sit here and drink my coffee,
And the realization slowly sets in.

~Waxing Gibbous~

If I were the moon in the heavens,
And you were a mortal on earth,
If I whispered in your ear a confession,
Would you give to me your attention,
If I were the moon in the heavens,
And you were a mortal on earth?

If I were the moon in her glory,
And you a fair mortal on earth,
Would you listen while I told you a story,
While you lay in the grass in uplands airy,
If I were the moon in her glory,
And you a fair mortal on earth?

If I were the moon in her kingdom,
And you my sweet mortal on earth,
Would you willingly be my Endymion,
My darling and slumbering Endymion,
If I were the moon in her kingdom,
And you my sweet mortal on earth?

~Full Moon~

I thrill to think of your hand in mine,
Of the warmth of your skin
Pressing into my own.
Something as simple as this…
It is enough to make me wonder,
Enough to stir the butterflies
Into a frenzy in my stomach.

~Waning Gibbous~

Something dormant lies within me,
Something calmly sleeping.
I wait with bated breathing
To feel it gently stir.
I suspect that when it wakes,
It will commence to feeding
On my energy, my being;
On my life force, as it were.

~Last Quarter~

Contained within an atom
Is the universe we know,
And every single atom
Is a universe of its own.

~Waning Crescent~

I am here, but barely,
Unnoticed in the sky.
Like a waning crescent moon
Looks down when the sun is high.
I am what you don't see...
Unless you look real close.
A specter in a sky so blue,
A dim outline at most.
But when the sun is gone;
When the sky turns black,
I will be the brightest light,
Among all the lights that lack.

~New Moon~

I journey inward.
You may wait here for my return,
But I cannot guarantee that it will be soon.
But if you do…
If you are still here when I emerge,
Do not expect to see the same person
Walking towards you.
For I will be different.
If you're at all unsure…
If at first your hand moves to the
Sword at your side,
And you peer at me wonderingly–
Questioningly,
I will not be offended.
Look into my eyes.
They will not have changed,

And when you look into them
You will know.

~Waxing Crescent~

And with the sun
Comes a new day,
And another attempt
To get it right.

~First Quarter~

This moment is pivotal,
For everything from now on,
Originates from here.

~Waxing Gibbous~

I stood on the edge of the world,
Just as the moon was eclipsed.
I had traveled so far,
And now I would know,
The answer to the riddle of the glyphs;
To the riddle of the runes and the glyphs.

Then suddenly I saw it,
In the shadow that covered the moon.
It revealed itself
And the meaning was clear,
The meaning of the riddle of the runes;
Of the riddle of the glyphs and the runes.

~Full Moon~

Tonight I will light a
Candle to your beauty,
A simple flame
In the hope that you will
Take note of me.
Oh take note
Of me!

~Waning Gibbous~

You watch and you know
The comings and goings,
Always watching
And knowing,
Yet you breathe not a word.

You have seen and you know
All that is happening.
Always seeing
And knowing
And not saying a word.

~Last Quarter~

Late at night
While the wind from the moor
Blew in through my window,
A bird stately and hoar,
Alighted on the sill and proceeded to
Speak with solemn vigor,

You know who I am,
You've heard of me before,
I have come from a far
Plutonian shore.
I see that you read
There a curious lore.

I say, What do you stare at
Me so ghastly for?
I will not utter
That word you abhor—
Have not uttered it
Since I rapped at that door;
That Ed, you know,
He was a nervous sort
Ever pining for that
Dead woman Lenore.

But ah, I am distracted,
It is YOU I'm here for!
Here he unrolled a paper
In his claw he had bore.

Forgive me, I am a
Daft bird of yore,
It seems the message
IS the very word you abhor!
The message simply is this–
NEVERMORE!

With that he abandoned
My window, I'm sure
To wing his way back
To Plutonian shores.
Now I'm left to wonder
And, what is more,
Pine for what I've lost
To reclaim nevermore!

~Waning Crescent~

I unraveled today.
I finally pulled on that loose string.
I lost all I had today.
Because it unwound everything.

Now here I sit in the quiet evening,
Naked and cold to the bone.
Because I pulled on the string
That should've been left alone.

~New Moon~

Crush the poppy in my drink.
I would quaff it and would sleep
Eternally, dreamless and deep.
Only to sleep, and not to think.

~Waxing Crescent~

It seems you've been gone forever.
In your absence I've nearly
Disappeared myself.
The light has burnt low,
It barely burns at all.
It's flickered a couple times.
I've never seen it do that.
I'm not sure I can carry it any further.
You waited too long to come back.

~First Quarter~

I sit and watch the sunrise,
And drink coffee,
And always get the feeling
That this is what I'll be
Doing at the end of the world.

~Waxing Gibbous~

Oh morning unparalleled
In beauty!
How you move a poet's soul
To benediction!

~Full Moon~

Look to her when you need me,
When you feel the old desire.
When you're saddened by my silence,
Look to her for comfort,
For she is me
And I am her,
And when you want me
She will be there.

~Waning Gibbous~

I walk the gardens at night,
For it is then that I find myself
Closer to the meaning of my memories.
When the wind is high and the moon
Is a silver orb peeking now and then
Through the clouds.
I walk noiselessly through the night
And the winding garden paths,
The scent of the night-flowers there
Bringing me closer to the secret of
My memories.
It is on a night like this that I
Feel I will remember.
Such a night as this, that will make
Everything clear.

~Last Quarter~

I have seen the future,
And it has left me feeling
Lonely.

~Waning Crescent~

I've struck out on a path of enlightenment
That will make my world darker,
Twirling my staff merrily
And humming a cheerful tune.
With manic abandon I do not fear the
Shadows that will soon surround me.
For such is the journey
For one who seeks the truth.

~New Moon~

My life is not my own,
It is borrowed;
Taken from somewhere
Beyond this place.

~Waxing Crescent~

The stars have cheered me,
Still I see in them
My demise.

~First Quarter~

When it was my turn to hear the learned
astronomer,
When the facts were given,
And much of what I thought I knew was
confirmed,
When my heart was reminded;
I shrank within myself,
Though before I had walked
Into the lecture-room
I had already felt small.

~Waxing Gibbous~

In last night's moonbeam I thought I saw you,
A pale form by the water's edge,
Tonight I've returned for I'm sure that I saw you,
And I wait to see if I can see you again.

I have dwelt in the cold, in the dark, in the cold.
My heart ceased to beat long ago when you left,
So tonight I've returned to wait and to hold,
To the hope of an image by the water's edge.

~Full Moon~

Dearest Luna,
Sweet mother and friend,
Thank you for existing
And for whatever it is you remind me
Of when I see you,
Thank you for that.

~Waning Gibbous~

There is one!
And another!
One,
Two,
Three,
Stars streak across the sky.
This is a rare opportunity,
A bounty for wishing!
I cannot help but smile.
Oh to be so young,
To believe in such things!

~Last Quarter~

Traveling on a lonely road that cut through
barren land,
I came upon a bent old woman, clutching a bag in
both her hands.
It was small and plain and brown, and seemed to
be quite full,
And the weight of it, on the woman, was clearly
taking its toll.
I asked her what she carried, and if I could carry
it for a while.
She replied, "It's my collection, and it's mine to
carry, child."
"What is it you collect?" I asked, for I couldn't
guess.
She looked at me with heavy eyes, and said, "I
collect regrets."
Surprised by her answer, I put my hand on her
frail shoulder.
"Why not drop the bag right here? Why carry it
any further?"
"Because this bag is my curse, and to carry it is
my fate.
To remind me of chances not taken, to remind me
of choices made."
I pondered that for a while, and when I finally
spoke,
I said, "It's not fair that you have one, when I
should have one of my own.

I too have made poor decisions, there are chances
I neglected to take,
I should be carrying a bag, and suffering too from
its weight."
She peered at me then very closely, squinting her
rheumy blue eyes.
"I think that you already do, child. You carry it
hidden inside."

~Waning Crescent~

The disease spread rapidly,
But it wasn't until it reached our souls,
That I knew it was over.

~New Moon~

On a cold night in November,
I walked the streets alone.
A forlorn, brooding wanderer,
With no appetite for home.

Up and down the streets were quiet
But for the leaves that noisily scurried,
Rushing before my trudging feet
In a desperate, frantic hurry.

I knew, this night, from what they fled.
I knew just what they feared.
The nameless shadow coming fast behind
That has followed me for years.

~Waxing Crescent~

Something calls to me of late.
I hear my name
Whispered in my ear.

~First Quarter~

Come, wander with me in quiet woodland ways,
Among trees as old as our souls.
Tell me of your life,
As we bask in a shaft of light,
You and I, philosophers of life and woodland
ways.

~Waxing Gibbous~

Meet me when the moon is full,
Let me take your hand.
Whisper why it is you came
I need to understand.

Do you want me? Tell me true
I feel I have to know,
If you are here because of life
Or are you sick of home?

~Full Moon~

Summer glided lazily by
And the world didn't see.
How could they have known
That it was I
Who lay dreaming within
The apple bower?

~Waning Gibbous~

Let's float this way for a while
'Til the evening shadows grow long,
And the willows on the bank,
With reaching tendrils,
Beckon us to return.
Let's sit like this for a while,
Musing on the ways
Of fate and love,
'Til the evening light
Begins to dwindle
And our hearts for home
Begin to yearn.

~Last Quarter~

In the middle of summer,
My heart felt like winter;
A cold draft swept the corridors
While I stood in the sun.

~Waning Crescent~

In the dark, the past crept up
And tapped me on the shoulder.
"Hello old friend."
It whispered in my ear.
I knew the voice.
I didn't reply.
I didn't say a word.
But tears began to silently fall.
"I have come to visit you, after all this time."
"Why? Why are you here?"
I asked, barely above a whisper.
"Because it is time."
I turned to look it straight in the face.
"Time for what?"
I saw it smile, through my tears.
"Time for us to make peace."

~New Moon~

In times archaic
I dwelled here,
After I'd ceased to roam.
These ghastly trees
I felled here,
To fashion myself a throne.
I ruled this
Little kingdom
With a supreme and iron hand,
Sharing arcane
Bits of wisdom
With those who could understand.
But my subjects were
Fickle and wild,
They ran about at their will,
And a few that
Had been exiled
Were found hanging around there still.
And I waited too long
To subdue them,
So one night they boldly rebelled,
And in a black rage
I slew them
And put on the land a spell.
Thereafter I sat
In the darkness,
And brooded on all that had passed.
'Neath a sky
Dismal and starless,

In my sorrow I sat, 'til at last,
I rose from my throne and departed,
Leaving the cursed land behind,
The land of the
Wild broken-hearted;
The land I had ruled in my mind.

~Waxing Crescent~

It seems I have sat here forever,
Waiting and watching the water,
Waiting for movement;
A stirring in the water,
Watching for an angel
To trouble the water.

~First Quarter~

Poke and prod and hit it again,
With chairs and whips you rabble-men.
Do so until you know it is dead,
This lion that's reared its menacing head.

~Waxing Gibbous~

My Mistress will soon
Enter her sable hall,
And I loiter in a corner,
Hoping to catch a glimpse of her,
My luminous lover.

~Full Moon~

Come with me,
Help me push this boat from the bank.
For tonight a moon-path lies across the water,
And it beckons for us to follow.

Sitting here in its glow,
Tell me, can you feel it?
The ethereal;
The climate of an other-world?

~Waning Gibbous~

A premonition plagues my mind,
A feeling on the wind.
Could it be that I imagine it?
Or that the wind is whispering a lie?
But a fear is growing upon me,
Heralded by the wind.
Aeolus, do you deceive me?
Is this trickery blown from your isle?

~Last Quarter~

I am heartened by you,
By the example that you set on a daily basis.
You are so full of kindness,
And compassion.
Even to strangers.
Even to those who are not kind in return.
I see you,
Though you don't realize that I do,
And am given hope.
I am given hope for the human race.
Please, don't ever stop.
Keep being kind.
It's all the world needs really.
It's what can save us.

~Waning Crescent~

And now I greet each dawn
With a feeling of expectancy;
A feeling of hope.
I am in constant awe of everything around me,
And my heart overflows.
How is it that I have lived so long
And only feel this way now?
I wonder, am I nearing death?

~New Moon~

Back to the old darkness.
I have dwelt in what
Has seemed like light,
Long enough.

~Waxing Crescent~

Life is so much time grasping at strands
And carefully weaving them
Into nice and neat plans,
But plans, if not tended to once they're begun,
Like braids in your hair that aren't
Tied at the ends,
Will loosen and fail and on their own
Come undone.

~First Quarter~

The signal was sent centuries ago,
From so far away, that it may not
Reach us for centuries yet.
Then again, perhaps it is close.
One thing is certain,
When it is received,
Everything as we know it will change.
The speculation will become reality.
I confess that I would find
It very entertaining should it
Happen during my lifetime.
I will watch it all unfold
With a knowing smile.

~Waxing Gibbous~

There are secrets
Waiting in places
I've never been;
Knowledge
In moments
I have yet to live.

~Full Moon~

At each turn, when the moon is full,
I lay out my obsidian mirror,
In the hopes that it
Will capture her reflection.
Oh pane of blackest sheen,
Has she ever caught a glimpse
Of herself in you?
Has she ever lingered for just a
Moment, in surprise of what
She saw?
Show her truly, oh mirror I beseech
You, show her as she is.
No ripple or fleeting shimmer to
Distort or obscure her visage.
For if she will but SEE,
But pause for a moment,
I will have her forever.

~Waning Gibbous~

If when you tell them that I am yours,
Your heart is not pleased,
Then I must be mine again.

~Last Quarter~

I weary of the world,
Of its hate,
And its ways.
Would that I could dwell on
The Peaks of Eternal Light
And watch the happenings
From afar.
I tire of being so small,
So quiet,
And ineffective.
I wish that I could sit in the
Silence of space,
And pen endless strings of words.
Not words to be remembered,
But words to be forgotten…
Words that will make myself and
My mortal woes forgotten.

~Waning Crescent~

I am drifting rudderless,
Without direction,
And I search for something
Irrevocably lost.

~New Moon~

An owl sat outside my window
The night my faith died,
A mournful witness to
An inevitable conclusion.

~Waxing Crescent~

I am not what you knew before,
For I died sometime in the night,
And this person before you now,
Is nothing more than a wight.

~First Quarter~

I have often felt that I don't belong,
Whether because of an
Overactive imagination,
Or because it is true,
I'm not altogether sure.
But I've always felt it,
And I've always wanted to know
What it'd be like to feel
Otherwise.

~Waxing Gibbous~

How easy it is to love you.
How effortless to be in your presence.
Even for one such as I,
Who never feels that love is easy.
How wonderful it is to give
Of my heart without complaining,
To love without resisting,
And want without restraining.

~Full Moon~

The day is gone,
The night is here.
It seeks to ensnare me,
I know that it does,
With its illusions
And trappings.
But I am not so easily fooled,
Not so naive as that.
I will not think that
The phantom I see out
Of the corner of my eye
Is my long-lost lover…
Will not believe that
In the shadow cast
From that tree
Someone stands.
I will not give in to
The dreaminess and
Fantastic visions
Caused by this strange lunar light.
I will keep my senses about me
As I cross this vague
And shadowy landscape.
I will make it to the morning
And the coming of the day,
Without falling victim
To this clever and sinister
Night.

~Waning Gibbous~

I've spent much of my life
In a corner,
Sitting alone and
Detached.
Detesting those who
Would speak,
Eyeing warily those who
Would pass.

~Last Quarter~

I am here,
Waiting,
Watching,
Withering.
Give me the signal,
The blessing,
Something,
Anything.

~Waning Crescent~

The candle is burning low,
But the shadows on the walls
Have not ceased to dance.
The candle has burned for hours,
But my heart feels there is
Time yet, that there is still a chance
You will come before it burns out,
That I will hear you down the hall,
That you will step into my room quietly,
While the shadows still dance the walls.

~New Moon~

I drift upon Lethean waters,
In search of oblivion
And eternal sleep.

~Waxing Crescent~

I only ask you this—
If I am suddenly missing one day,
Don't make it into a big affair.
Don't send out search parties,
Or have people looking.
Just know that I would've
Wanted to go out in a quiet way.
Go ahead and arrange the funeral,
And don't worry that I may yet show up.
I won't care who was there and who wasn't.
I could only count on a few anyway.
If I am suddenly missing one day,
Then I am gone,
And put on my stone this simple epitaph—
ALIVE IN DEATH.

~First Quarter~

I sometimes wonder if you
See in me what others do not,
And then I wonder when you will.

~Waxing Gibbous~

Equinox is a time for meeting,
So come to me then
And deep within a lynx's den
We'll light a fire and drink to health,
And I'll tell you of what befell
That cast me from among my kind
And sent me into long exile.

It is a tale dark and fell
That I will sit and tell you,
A tale of shadows
And forbidden things.

The fire will help to strengthen our courage
And the drink will help to forget our fears;
But the lynx will sit at the entrance and watch.

~Full Moon~

I know not how this will end,
But I know that it will.
Everything ends in the end you know.
But I guess we can walk for a while together,
Walk and talk until then.
We can walk and talk and maybe love,
At least until it ends.

~Waning Gibbous~

At midday I ran with a Sundog,
But tonight I shall run with the Overdog;
Run and howl with the Overdog,
Across the great span of the sky.

At midday I ran with the sun,
But tonight I shall run with the stars;
Whoop and holler among the stars,
And chase the joyful reply.

~Last Quarter~

In your arms
I learned what
It was like to
Feel whole and
Broken at the
Same time.

~Waning Crescent~

In the black depths it was
Revealed to me,
The secret I had sought.

~New Moon~

I dreamt of another world;
Of pillars made of cloud
And chasms filled with stars.
I was flying at night,
In an ethereal sky,
Alone but for the company
Of an alien moon.

I was snug inside my little machine,
But a strange music hummed without.
It seemed to surround and press
On all sides,
As though bearing my plane
On a river of sound.

Hypnotic, it lulled my mind to sleep,
Quieting the vague alarm
That had surfaced.
It wasn't until it was too
Late that I realized
I was no longer alone.

~Waxing Crescent~

This day is warm,
But I am chilled to the marrow,
For it has visited me again,
The harbinger from the barrow;
The dreaded reaper grim.

~First Quarter~

I find that I want to write you
Love letters in the guise
Of something else.
Hidden within the vague ideas of
Ordinary poems,
Between obscure lines,
I want to give you my heart.

~Waxing Gibbous~

Oh that reality had not taken
Its imposing throne,
But that imagination could have
Reigned and ruled forever!

~Full Moon~

Something is out there.
It waits for me,
Just outside the circle of light.

~Waning Gibbous~

I walk when the town is asleep,
And the lights in the windows are out.
I walk to the bridge that crosses
The river.
I stop in the middle and rest my elbows
On the rail.
There is something about it at night.
You can FEEL the water rushing below
Though you cannot see it.
It always fills me with a curious
Sense of longing,
And every night I must fight the
Urge to jump.

~Last Quarter~

I can't shake this mood…
I think I need to run away
And get lost in a place
Where I do not have a name,
And am not expected to.

~Waning Crescent~

I looked inside of another.
I saw what resided within.
It wasn't what I'd expected.
It wasn't anything like their skin.
It wasn't like their outside at all.
Their body gave no indication,
That the thing that I saw when I looked inside,
To the outside had no correlation.

~New Moon~

The walls of my mind
Are hung with tapestries,
Decorated with the scenes
It loves the best...
The memories it cherishes most.
Woven threads of colors rich and bright,
From a time when life was brighter.
Scenes woven on a magical loom,
To a background of laughter
And happy child's play.
When I am alone,
I often look at these scenes adorning
My walls.
I run my fingers along their textures,
And remember.
I look at them,
And mourn.

~Waxing Crescent~

The wind blows
And never yields,
And ripples of silver
Dance on the fields.
This is summer
In the land of plenty,
Of beans and corn,
And milk and honey.

~First Quarter~

The sunlight around the
Edge of the curtain
This morning reminded
Me of you;
The birds singing
Their early morning
Songs.
I am reminded of you
At random times,
And the memory is
Always accompanied
By a sharp and
Sudden pang.

~Waxing Gibbous~

And what will any of this mean
Years from now,
After the mountains have been
Worn down to nothing more
Than hills,
And the sea has risen to
Cover them?
What will the memories made today
Represent for us tomorrow?
Who will care then what is written
On a stone slab?
Tell me that this will all
Mean something in the end,
When it is all said and done.
Tell me that the time we
Spend together now,
Will be precious to us forever.

~Full Moon~

I looked at you.
REALLY LOOKED at you,
And to my surprise
I recognized myself.
Your scars...
They were like my own.
Your expression,
One of sorrow,
Just like mine.
And when I discovered that
You knew me,
That you had been watching me,
That you loved me already...
Well, in that moment,
I felt like I had found home.
Like I had found where
I belonged.
Since then,
You have become everything to me.
You gave me a piece of
Yourself...
And it has saved my life.
I owe you everything,
My friend.
My darling.
My love.

~Waning Gibbous~

It has taken all this time
For me to finally want to be here.
Not to simply accept that I'm
Here, but to actually WANT to
Be here.
I do not want to die.
I want to live.
More than anything,
I want to live.

~Last Quarter~

My life is measured by two
Glass bulbs,
Carefully curved and accurate
To a fault.
When I close my eyes and listen,
I can hear the granules sliding
Together and falling into a
Collective heap.
My moments are measured by this,
This cleverly designed
Contraption,
This haunting reminder of time...
And I know that the sand is
Slipping faster now
Through its narrow neck.

~Waning Crescent~

It is time.
My craft is ready, as am I.
T-minus ten…nine…
Bound for climes Elysian,
I'm grateful for time given.
Eight…seven…
I give this message to mankind,
And to those I leave behind,
Six…five…
Life is more than what you see.
What you are now, you won't always be.
Four…three…
Farewell my fleeting home.
The adventure has only begun.
Two…one…

LIFTOFF